CU00793510

Trier Travel Highlights

Best Attractions & Experiences

Jacqueline McCulloch

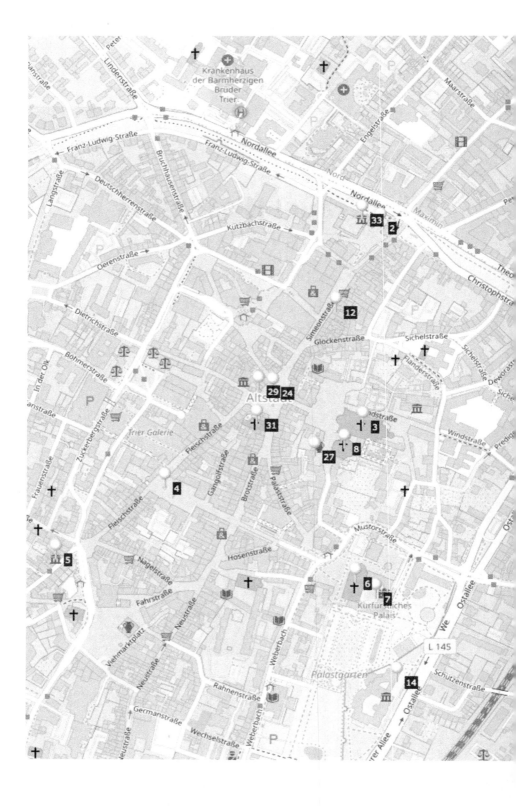

Contents

Welcome to Trier

Set in the beautiful Moselle wine region of Germany close to Luxembourg, the city of Trier is a popular destination for wine-lovers and history buffs. Its historic center is one of Germany's finest—Roman ruins grace the city center, and a handful of historical monuments help bring to life the city's medieval past. Trier was the birthplace of Karl Marx. Once the capital of the Western Roman Empire, it has a medieval old town filled with half-timbered houses.

□ 1. Kaiserthermen

Address: 49 Weberbach, Trier 54290, Germany

Immerse yourself in a little history at the Kaiserthermen, Trier. Boasting a unique octagonal design and stretching back as far as 1650 BC, this ancient bathhouse was once used as a gathering place for the local villagers to come together and socialize. While those ancient times may be gone, locals and tourists still return to enjoy a visit to this remarkable structure.

□ 2. Porta Nigra City Gate

Address: Porta-Nigra-Platz, 54290 Trier, Germany
Web: http://www.trier-info.de/portanigra-info

The Porta Nigra (or black gate) is a large Roman city gate in Trier. It is today the largest Roman city gate north of the Alps. The name Porta Nigra originated in the Middle Ages due to the darkened colour of its stone; the original Roman name has not been preserved.

□ 3. High Cathedral of St Peter

Web: http://www.dominformation.de/

The High Cathedral of Saint Peter (Trier Cathedral), is a three-naved Romanesque church. It was built from 1030 to 1250 and is the oldest church in Germany whose architectural features have been largely preserved. The cathedral is notable for its long life span – the central part of the nave was built between about 520 and 550 – and its grand yet sympathetic design. With a length of 150 metres and a width of 50 metres, it covers a larger area than many cathedrals.

☐ 4. Sankt Georgsbrunnen

Address: 4 Kornmarkt, Trier 54290, Germany

The Sankt Georgsbrunnen in Trier dates back to the 12th century. It was enclosed in a tower beside the town hall from 1897 to 1949 to protect it from vandals. Repairs were necessary as a result of the damages done by bombings during World War II. In 1949 it was restored to its current place near the Municipal Museum and is still functional today.

☐ 5. Karl Marx House

Phone: +49 651 970680

Web: http://www.museum-karl-marx-haus.de/

The Karl Marx House Museum in Trier is the former residence of Karl Marx, co-founder of communism. It is situated on what used to be the Brüderstrasse ("Brothers Street"), where he lived at No. 4 from 1839 until his death in 1883. The museum consists of the middle-class five-story Würzburger Hof with the main wing facing the city's park, and the low Rheinische Weinhandlung (Rhenish Wine Shop) adjacent to it which housed his office.

□ 6. Aula Palatina Basilica

Address: Konstantinplatz 10, 54290 Trier, Germany
Phone: +49 651 994 91200
Email: ev-gemeinde.trier@ekkt.de
Web: http://www.konstantin-basilika.de/

The Aula Palatina, also called Basilica of Constantine, was commissioned by the emperor at the beginning of the 4th century. It is one of the largest surviving Roman structures built for imperial purposes, and was one of the architectural elements of the tetrarchic palace city on the Palatine Hill in Rome. The 2nd-floor basilica was used for ceremonial receptions and official business, while the ground floor with its 100 columns was reserved for the private use of emperor and court. To this day it remains one of the best preserved buildings from antiquity. It is a UNESCO World Heritage Site.

□ 7. Kurfürstliches Palais

The Kurfürstliches Palais is a Baroque palace in Trier. It was built between 1690 and 1730 for Elector Palatine Charles III William (the last ruler of the independent Duchy of Pfalz) and served as his primary residence for most of the period from 1699 to his death in 1738. From 1799 to 1918 the building was the residence of Prussian kings Frederick William III and Wilhelm I. After both kings died in this palace it became a state museum in 1918.

□ 8. Church of Our Lady

Address: Liebfrauenstraße 1, 54290 Trier, Germany
Web: http://www.liebfrauen-trier.de

Built between 1010 and 1047 the Frauenkirche or Church of Our Lady, is among the earliest churches built in the Gothic style. It contains elements of classic French Gothic architecture which was popularised during the reign of King Henry II of France.

☐ 9. Igeler Säule Pillar Tomb

Address: 39 Trierer Straße, Igel 54298, Germany

The Igeler Säule is the largest existing pillar tomb in Germany. A family shown on the grave was for centuries misinterpreted as showing the marriage of the parents of the Emperor Constantine and prevented the Roman monument from being destroyed. The 23 metre Igeler Säule pillar is on the UNESCO World Cultural Heritage list.

☐ 10. Roman Bridge

Address: Römerbrücke, Trier 54294, Germany

Considered one of the most beautiful Roman bridges in the world, the Roman Bridge in Trier is almost 2,000 years old. Built in AD 160, it's the oldest standing bridge in Germany. Measuring 684 feet, this majestic structure stretches across the Moselle River. Heavily used until modern times, The Roman Bridge became a symbol of European unity following World War II. Still used to this day for pedestrian and automobile traffic, it's 260 feet upstream from Moselle's Neumarkt Bridge.

☐ 11. Amphitheater

The Amphitheater, Trier is an ancient monument that was used for gladiatorial contests and public spectacles, much like the Colosseum in Rome. Although it wasn't "built" until the early 2nd century A.D. by the Romans, there had been a theater here since 50 B.C., so it is almost as old as the famous Roman monument to the emperor.

☐ 12. Dreikönigenhaus

The Dreikönigenhaus, Trier is a 10 bedroom, 13 bathroom house built by Frederick of Prussia in the year 1701. This French Baroque Style House has beautiful interior features such as an early, richly decorated Rococo style ceiling, wall paintings on 18 painted panels and open stucco work composed of gold and white. This architectural piece is one of the most important Renaissance monuments in Rhineland-Palatinate and is classified as one of the National Monuments of Germany.

□ 13. Trier Bridge

Address: Kaiser-Wilhelm-Brücke, Trier 54292, Germany

Located in the heart of the central German town of Trier, the Kaiser-Wilhelm-Brücke (also known as the Trier Bridge) offers both pedestrians and vehicles a route across the Moselle River.

□ 14. Rhinish Regional Museum

Address: Weimarer Allee 1, 54290 Trier, Germany

Phone: +49 651 97740

Email: landesmuseum-trier@gdke.rlp.de

The Rheinische Landesmuseum is an archaeological museum in Trier. The museum's collections cover the prehistory of the local area, including Gallo-Roman culture in Trier and the Moselle region. The antique collection (Museum der Antike) includes Roman art from Augustus to Constantine I, sarcophagi and Roman sculptures.

□ 15. St. Matthias Abbey

Address: Matthiasstraße 85, 54290 Trier, Germany

Phone: +49 651 17090

Email: Benediktiner@AbteiStMatthias.de

Web: http://www.abteistmatthias.de/

The abbey church, a Romanesque basilica, is a renowned place of pilgrimage because of the tomb of St. Matthias the Apostle (he succeeded Judas Iscariot), after whom the abbey is named, located here since the 12th century. St. Matthew's Abbey is the only burial site that includes an Apostle north of the Alps. The first monastery was built around 480 by followers of St. Matthias's disciple St. Valerius, making it Westphalia's oldest religious house.

☐ 16. Roscheider Hof Open Air Museum

Address: Roscheiderhof 1, 54329 Konz, Germany
Phone: +49 6501 92710
Email: info@RoscheiderHof.de
Web: http://www.roscheiderhof.de/

The Roscheider Hof Open Air Museum is housed in the former farmstead of Roscheider Hof in Konz. It is a museum covering the rural and farming history of northwest Rhineland-Palatinate and the German-Luxembourg-Lorraine border region.

□ 17. Barbarathermen

Address: 48 Südallee, Trier 54290, Germany

The Barbarathermen, Trier is an important and geographically isolated Roman aqueduct. This unique waterworks system provides us with insight into Roman technology and city planning as well as on the development of the city of Trier.

□ 18. Burg Heid

Address: 1 Burg Heid, Burg Heid 54429, Germany

The Burg Heid is a castle located in Trier. The castle is situated above the town on a strategic rocky outcrop. Lying along the Mosel River, the Burg has served many purposes over its lifetime. For over 1,000 years, it served as a residence for local nobility. During World War II, the Burg was used as a base for German soldiers. Today, it is considered a "green fortress" because of the many environmentally friendly elements added to the structure.

□ 19. Irsch Wine Region

Wikipedia: https://en.wikipedia.org/wiki/Irsch

Irsch is an municipality in Rhineland-Palatinate near to Trier, most famous for its viticulture. With over 20 wine producers, the village has recently become known for its Riesling wines. It is located near the border with Luxembourg in an area with thousands of years of history.

☐ 20. Burg Castle Museum

Web: https://kulturdb.de/einobjekt.php?id=1095

The Burg Sommerau is located on the Moselle River. Its castle was originally built around 1000 AD. The castle served as protection for German Emperors during the Middle Ages. Its attached monastery contained a large library which was closed in 1574 on the order of Martin Luther during the Reformation Wars. Today, it is a fully-restored castle and museum open to tourists.

☐ 21. Drachenhaus

Address: 5 Stuckradweg, 54293, Germany

The Drachenhaus was once a dragon house built in 850 AD by the ruler of the area, Count Lambert. Destroyed during a siege by the French in 1657. Now a tourist attraction and hotel/restaurant near Trier.

☐ 22. Schloss Saarstein Winery

Address: 1 Schloss Saarstein, 54455, Germany
Web: http://www.saarstein.de/

Schloss Saarstein is a family-owned winery. The Schloss was built in 1423, and has been in operation since 1003 when Emperor Otto III granted a farm to the Abbey of St. Matthias in Trier, which would later become Hermann-Joseph University. Since then, there have been almost one hundred cellar masters who have passed on their vintner's skills down through seven generations of winemakers at Schloss Saarstein.

□ 23. Schloss Saarfels

Schloss Saarfels is a castle in Trier. It was built following the early Gothic architectural style between 1247 and 1250. The castle was destroyed in 1554 and was rebuilt in the 17th century.

☐ 24. Hauptmarkt

Address: 16 Hauptmarkt, Trier 54290, Germany

The Hauptmarkt is Trier's main market square. It's a bustling, vibrant place in the heart of the city. Located in a maze of historic pathways in the center of Trier, the Hauptmarkt is a popular hang out spot for locals and visitors alike. The large space is lined with locally-oriented cafes, restaurants, shops and hotels catering to a wide range of tastes. At one end is a towering cathedral that towers overhead, while at the other end an array of medieval buildings still in use today surround the square.

☐ 25. Burg Ramstein

Address: 3 Burg Ramstein, 54306, Germany

Burg Ramstein castle was built in the 1140s. It was a simple three-story tower surrounded by a rectangular curtain wall. In the 14th century, a residential tower called "Münzturm" was added on top of the main tower. In 1332, Burg Ramstein became the property of the Counts of Sponheim who then built out the structure into a stronger fortress.

□ 26. Schusterkreuz Cross

The Schusterkreuz is a wayside cross located in Trier, 20 km (12 miles) west of Luxembourg City.

□ 27. Weinstube Kesselstatt

Phone: +49 651 41178

Email: info@weinstube-kesselstatt.de

Web: http://www.weinstube-kesselstatt.de/

Weinstube Kesselstatt is an urban wine tavern located in the old city of Trier on the banks of the Moselle. It is a pleasant atmosphere for wine-tasting (where you can taste the wine straight from the barrel) with seating areas by day and at night.

□ 28. Burg Grimburg

Burg Grimburg, Trier Often referred to as "The Burg" by locals, this fortress dates back to the 12th century. Constructed by the ruling family of Luxembourg, who later became the ruling family of The Netherlands and Belgium, The Burg served both as a fortress to deter attacks and contain unruly populations within its walls. Then in the 1800s it served as a prison for captured

French soldiers who had attempted to invade Germany during the Napoleonic Wars. Currently the Burg is home to restaurants, shops and museums.

□ 29. Steipe Building

Wikipedia: https://de.wikipedia.org/wiki/Steipe

The Steipe is a Gothic building on the main market square in Trier. It is a favorite gathering place for students during the day.

☐ 30. Schloss Quint

Built at the end of the 16th century, Schloss Quint, Trier is a rare example of a castle that combines Renaissance and Gothic elements. The design features a stunning three-storey Renaissance arcade with a three-story tower. The interiors include beautiful Rococo decorations and tapestries from the 19th century. This building has been restored to its original beauty and is now available for sale, as well as for public tours.

☐ 31. Saint Gangolf's Church

St. Gangolf's Church is an early Romanesque basilica located in Trier. Constructed in the 10th century, it is the city's oldest existing building. St. Gangolf's is recognized as a Roman Catholic Church of historical significance and enjoys protection under German law. It was built adjacent to the remains of a Roman camp that dates back to at least the 2nd century AD.

☐ 32. St. Paulin Church

A little further out from the centre of Trier, the Paulin Kirche is worth a visit. The baroque interior is beautiful, with white and gold illuminations. In the crypt you can see the graves of the martyrs of Trier.

☐ 33. Stadtmuseum Simeonstift

Phone: +49 651 7181459

Web: http://www.museum-trier.de/

The Simeonstift in Germany was founded in 1009 and is one of the oldest and most important ecclesiastical foundations in the German state of Rhineland-Palatinate. The museum in Trier covers almost 900 years of church history, from the Early Middle Ages to the present day. It holds a wide range of works such as medieval liturgical art such as crucifixes and reliquaries, altars and sculptures, paintings and mosaics from bygone eras, all kinds of book art such as Bibles and prayer books, musical instruments, jewellery and costumes.

☐ 34. Cable Car Station

Address: 44 Erdenbach, Saarburg 54439, Germany

The Cable Car Station, Trier is located next to the Porta Nigra. It's one of Trier's most popular tourist destinations. The Cable Car has been operating since 1888 and offers travelers a panoramic view of the city.

☐ 35. Fell Exhibition Slate Mine

Phone: +49 65 02 99 40 19
Email: bergwerk-fell@t-online.de
Web: http://www.bergwerk-fell.de/

Fell Exhibition Slate Mine, Trier dates back to the Middle Ages and overlooks the Moselle River. The now-disused mine was once the largest in Europe and provided high-quality roofing slate for centuries. The underground tour takes you 30 meters below ground where you will discover how slate mining developed to its current state in the museum. You will also visit a winery and see wine making in action; the winery is located in the mine itself and has been operating since 1657.

Picture Credits

Trier, Germany Cover: analogicus / 5341262 (Pixabay)
Kaiserthermen: Berthold Werner (CC BY-SA 3.0)
Porta Nigra City Gate: Cthoe (CC BY-SA 3.0)
High Cathedral of St Peter: Albionhajdari (CC BY-SA 3.0)
Sankt Georgsbrunnen: Berthold Werner (CC BY-SA 3.0)
Karl Marx House: Berthold Werner (CC BY-SA 3.0)
Aula Palatina Basilica: Berthold Werner (PD)

Kurfürstliches Palais: Stefan Kühn (CC-BY-SA-3.0)

Church of Our Lady: Lokilech (CC BY-SA 3.0)

Igeler Säule Pillar Tomb: Berthold Werner (CC BY-SA 3.0)

Roman Bridge: Moritz Post (CC BY-SA 3.0)

Amphitheater: Stefan Kühn (CC-BY-SA-3.0)

Dreikönigenhaus: Eifeljanes (CC BY-SA 3.0)

Trier Bridge: Stefan Kühn (CC-BY-SA-3.0)

Rhinish Regional Museum: Stefan Kühn (CC-BY-SA-3.0)

St. Matthias Abbey: Stefan Kühn (CC-BY-SA-3.0)

Barbarathermen: Alexandre Wiltheim (10 Octobre, 1604 - 15 August, 1684) (PD)

Burg Heid: Wolkenkratzer (CC BY-SA 4.0)

Irsch Wine Region: Arno Meyer (PD)

Drachenhaus: Berthold Werner (CC BY-SA 3.0)

Schloss Saarstein Winery: Epei (CC-BY-SA-3.0)

Hauptmarkt: Berthold Werner (CC BY-SA 3.0)

Burg Ramstein: Brbbl (CC BY-SA 3.0)

Burg Grimburg: Palatinatian (CC BY-SA 2.5)

Steipe Building: Berthold Werner (CC BY-SA 3.0)

Schloss Quint: Berthold Werner (PD)

Saint Gangolf's Church: Berthold Werner (PD)

St. Paulin Church: Merian, Matthäus (PD)

Stadtmuseum Simeonstift: Stadtmuseum Simeonstift (CC BY-SA 3.0)

Printed in Great Britain
by Amazon